I have a dream that one day . . .
little black boys and black girls
will be able to join hands with
little white boys and white girls
as sisters and brothers.
I have a dream today!

—Dr. Martin Luther King Jr.
August 28, 1963

To my granddaughter, Farris Christine Watkins,
and all the other children of the world
who will continue my brother's dream of turning the world upside down—*C. K. F.*

my brother
MARTIN

A SISTER REMEMBERS
GROWING UP WITH THE REV. DR. MARTIN LUTHER KING JR.

BY CHRISTINE KING FARRIS

ILLUSTRATED BY CHRIS SOENTPIET

SIMON & SCHUSTER BOOKS FOR YOUNG READERS

New York   London   Toronto   Sydney   Singapore

Gather around and listen
as I share childhood memories of my brother,
the Reverend Dr. Martin Luther King Jr.
I am his older sister and
I've known him longer than anyone else.
I knew him long before the speeches he gave
and the marches he led
and the prizes he won.

I even knew him *before* he first dreamed *the* dream
that would change the world.

We were born in the same room,
my brother Martin and I.
I was an early baby,
born sooner than expected.
Mother Dear and Daddy placed me in
the chifforobe drawer that stood
in the corner of their upstairs bedroom.
I got a crib a few days afterward.
A year and a half later,
Martin spent his first night
in that hand-me-down crib
in the very same room.

The house where we were born
belonged to Mother Dear's parents,
our grandparents,
the Reverend and Mrs. A. D. Williams.
We lived there with them and our Aunt Ida,
our grandmother's sister.

And not long after my brother Martin—
who we called M. L.
because he and Daddy had the same name—
our baby brother was born.
His name was Alfred Daniel,
but we called him A. D., after our grandfather.

They called me Christine,
and like three peas in one pod,
we grew together.
Our days and rooms were filled
with adventure stories and Tinkertoys,
with dolls and Monopoly and Chinese checkers.

And although Daddy,
who was an important minister,
and Mother Dear,
who was known far and wide as a musician,
often had work that took them away from home,
our grandmother was always there to take care of us.
I remember days sitting at her feet,
as she and Aunt Ida filled us
with grand memories of their childhood
and read to us
about all the wonderful places in the world.

And of course, my brothers and I had each other.
We three stuck together
like the pages in a brand-new book.
And being normal young children,
we were almost *always* up to something.

Our best prank involved a fur piece
that belonged to our grandmother.
It looked almost alive,
with its tiny feet and little head
and gleaming glass eyes.
So, every once in a while,
in the waning light of evening,
we'd tie that fur piece to a stick,
and, hiding behind the hedge in front of our house,
we would dangle it
in front of unsuspecting passersby.
Boy! You could hear the screams of fright
all across the neighborhood!

Then there was the time Mother Dear
decided that her children should all learn to play piano.
I didn't mind too much,
but M. L. and A. D. preferred being outside
to being stuck inside with our piano teacher, Mr. Mann,
who would rap your knuckles with a ruler
just for playing the wrong notes.
Well, one morning,
M. L. and A. D. decided to loosen the legs
on the piano bench
so we wouldn't have to practice.
We didn't tell Mr. Mann,
and when he sat . . . *CRASH!*
down he went.

But mostly we were good, obedient children,
and M. L. did learn to play a few songs on the piano.
He even went off to sing with our mother
a time or two.
Given his love for singing and music,
I'm sure he could have become
as good a musician as our mother
had his life not called him down a different path.

But that's just what his life did.

My brothers and I grew up a long time ago.
Back in a time when certain places in our country had unfair laws
that said it was right to keep black people separate
because our skin was darker
and our ancestors had been captured in far-off Africa
and brought to America as slaves.

Atlanta, Georgia,
the city in which we were growing up, had those laws.
Because of those laws, my family rarely went to the picture shows
or visited Grant Park with its famous Cyclorama.
In fact, to this very day
I don't recall ever seeing my father on a streetcar.
Because of those laws,
and the indignity that went with them,
Daddy preferred keeping M. L., A. D., and me
close to home,
where we'd be protected.

We lived in a neighborhood in Atlanta
that's now called Sweet Auburn.
It was named for Auburn Avenue,
the street that ran in front of our house.
On our side of the street stood two-story frame houses
similar to the one we lived in.
Across it crouched a line of one-story row houses
and a store owned by a white family.

When we were young
all the children along Auburn Avenue played together,
even the two boys whose parents owned the store.

And since our house was a favorite gathering place,
those boys played with us in our backyard . . .

. . . and ran with M. L. and A. D.
to the firehouse on the corner
where they watched the engines and the firemen.

The thought of *not* playing with those kids
because they were different,
because they were white and we were black,
never entered our minds.

Well, one day, M. L. and A. D.
went to get their playmates from across the street
just as they had done a hundred times before.
But they came home alone.
The boys had told my brothers
that they couldn't play together anymore
because A. D. and M. L. were Negroes.

And that was it.
Shortly afterward the family sold the store
and moved away.
We never saw or heard from them again.

Looking back, I realize that it was only a matter of time
before the generations of cruelty and injustice
that Daddy and Mother Dear
and Mama and Aunt Ida
had been shielding us from
finally broke through.
But back then
it was a crushing blow
that seemed to come out of nowhere.

"Why do white people treat colored people so mean?"
M. L. asked Mother Dear afterward.
And with me and M. L. and A. D. standing in front of her
trying our best to understand,
Mother Dear gave the reason behind it all.

Her words explained
the streetcars our family avoided
and the WHITES ONLY sign
that kept us off the elevator at City Hall.
Her words told why there were parks and museums
that black people could not visit
and why some restaurants refused to serve us
and why hotels wouldn't give us rooms
and why theaters would only allow us to watch
their picture shows
from the balcony.

But her words also gave us hope.

She answered simply,
"Because they just don't understand
that everyone is the same,
but someday, it will be better."

And my brother M. L.
looked up into our mother's face
and said the words I remember to this day.

He said, "Mother Dear, one day
I'm going to turn this world upside down."

In the coming years
there would be other reminders
of the cruel system
called segregation
that sought to keep black people down.
But it was Daddy who showed
M. L. and A. D. and me how to
speak out against hatred and bigotry
and stand up for what's right.

Daddy was the minister at Ebenezer Baptist Church.
And after losing our playmates,
when M. L., A. D., and I
heard our father speak from his pulpit,
his words held new meaning.

And Daddy practiced what he preached.
He always stood up for himself
when confronted with hatred and bigotry,
and each day he shared his encounters
at the dinner table.

When a shoe salesman told Daddy and M. L.
that he'd only serve them in the back of the store
because they were black,
Daddy took M. L. somewhere else
to buy new shoes.

Another time, a police officer
pulled Daddy over and called him "boy."
Daddy pointed to M. L. sitting next to him in the car and said,
"This is a boy. I am a man,
and until you call me one,
I will not listen to you."

These stories were as nourishing
as the food that was set before us.

Years would pass,
and many new lessons would be learned.
There would be numerous speeches
and marches
and prizes.
But my brother never forgot
the example of our father,
or the promise he had made to our mother
on the day his friends turned him away.

And when he was much older,
my brother M. L. dreamed a dream . . .

. . . that turned the world upside down.

You Can Be Like Martin A Tribute to Dr. Martin Luther King Jr.

By Mildred D. Johnson

Martin was a peaceful boy,
And peaceful when a man.
He wanted peace for everyone
All throughout our land.
You can be a peaceful child,
Even a peaceful man.

You can be like Martin,
Yes, you can!

Martin was an intelligent boy,
Intelligent when a man.
He wanted good schools for everyone,
All throughout our land.

You can be an intelligent child,
Even an intelligent man.

You can be like Martin,
Yes, you can!

Martin was a proud boy,
And proud when he 'came a man.
He tried to teach pride to Black people,
All throughout our land.

You can be a proud child,
And proud when you're a man.

You can be like Martin,
Yes, you can!

Martin was a reading boy,
Kept reading when a man.
He knew good readers were needed,
All throughout our land.

You can be a reader,
Read on when you're a man.

You can be like Martin,
Yes, you can!

Martin was a speaking boy,
Kept speaking when a man.
His words touched many listeners,
All throughout our land.

You can be a speaker,
Speak on when you're a man.

You can be like Martin,
Yes, you can!

Martin was a praying boy,
How he prayed when he was a man.
He prayed that men would do right deeds,
All throughout our land.

You can pray in your own way,
Pray more when you're a man.

You can be like Martin,
Yes, you can!

Martin had a dream, you know,
That all people would be free,
To live and work together,
In a country filled with peace.

You can be a dreamer,
Keep dreaming when a man.

You can be like Martin,
Yes, you can!

Martin Luther King was a warrior of love,
A kind and loving man.
He wanted all to be loving,
All throughout our land.

You can be kind and loving,
Grow to a loving man.

You can be like Martin,
Yes, you can!

Martin Luther King sang, "We Shall Overcome,"
Sang it throughout our land.
You can overcome, my children,
Yes, you can!

You can be like Martin,
Yes, you can!

You *can* be like Martin,
Yes, you can!

You can be like Martin,
Yes, you can!

AFTERWORD

This book is written as an accurate reflection of the childhood experiences of my brother Martin; the late Rev. Dr. Martin Luther King Jr. Although many stories have been told about Martin's childhood, this one is firsthand. As the sole survivor of the family into which Martin Luther King Jr. was born, I feel it is important to share some true, funny, intriguing elements of Martin's earlier days. No other document can share this true story.

Many see Martin as a very serious-minded individual, stiff-necked, and always focused. What has not been emphasized enough is that Martin was once a boy. He, like others, developed gradually. He was funny. He was curious. He liked to play. He was a regular "fella."

I wanted to reflect another side of Martin's life story. The days that I spent with him, watching him, as we grew older, were valuable and meaningful exercises for me. They set him on his ultimate course. He indeed became a world leader. His contribution to the world cannot be denied or ignored and it is important for young people to realize the potential that lies within each of them to do this and greater works. I believe that a poem by Mildred D. Johnson entitled, "You Can Be Like Martin," reflects my feeling in this regard.

The highlight of the book, I think, is the moment that Martin expressed his commitment to affect change. Perhaps the information contained in this book will inspire young people to also become leaders of the future.

Aside from my memories of Martin's earlier years, I owe it to him to tell the full story. We had a great time as kids. I miss those days. The memories that I share here help to bring those times back and ensure that they are available for generations to come.

Christine King Farris, June 2002

Above photograph of author with her brother Martin Luther King Jr. taken in 1930; the background photograph was taken in 1935 when King was six years old.

For those who continue to preserve the legacy of Dr. King's dream—*C. S.*

ILLUSTRATOR'S NOTE

In May of 1999, while making a presentation for the International Reading Association in San Diego, California, I had the honor and pleasure of being introduced to Mrs. Christine King Farris. She attended my presentation and afterward asked me if I would be interested in working with her on a project—a book about her childhood with her brother, the late Dr. Martin Luther King. I was incredibly flattered. As a youngster, I had idolized this remarkable human being.

Mrs. Farris and I kept in contact, and before long, her editor at Simon & Schuster contacted me. Within a matter of days *My Brother Martin* was underway. My first course of action was a trip to the King Center in Atlanta, Georgia, where Mrs. Farris, our editor, and I walked through the places of Dr. King's childhood—his childhood home at 501 Auburn Avenue, Ebenezer Baptist Church, where he and his father served as minister, and even the neighborhood firehouse, where he and his friends spent much of their time. I snapped photographs and listened while Mrs. Farris regaled us with recollections of a very playful—and sometimes mischievous—little boy who would grow up to change the world. I was moved beyond words and left Atlanta with the feeling of being a part of something historic. A few months later, after the manuscript was completed, I took a second trip from New York City to Atlanta. This time I brought my studio with me—cameras, lighting equipment,

backdrop, and costumes—in preparation for an extensive model shoot. Mrs. Farris, the epitome of Southern graciousness and charm, greeted me at Ebenezer Baptist Church. There she had gathered models she had personally chosen to bring her memories to life.

The boys who pose as Martin Jr. and A. D., are both Mrs. Farris's great-nephews. Mrs. Farris's daughter—Dr. King's niece—portrays "Mother Dear," Dr. King's mother. The assistant pastor at Ebenezer Baptist Church portrays "Daddy" King. Even Christine's young granddaughter was an eager model and portrays a young Christine. The rest of the cast were personal and close friends of the King family. Many shared stories of their time with Dr. King, "M. L.," as they refer to him. And each agreed their participation was a great tribute to the King family and their legacy.

The spirit and generosity of Mrs. Farris, the staff at both the Ebenezer Baptist Church and the National Historic Site, and the King family helped to make my work on *My Brother Martin* as genuine as I think possible. It is my hope that the part I played in the creation of this book helps Dr. King's vision of justice and harmony live on and on.

Chris Soentpiet
June 2002 • New York, NY

Mrs. Farris's Acknowledgments: This book would not have been possible without the encouragement of my loving and devoted husband, Isaac Farris Sr., and my precious children, Isaac Farris Jr. and Dr. Angela Farris Watkins. Because of their abiding spirits, I acknowledge my parents, Martin Luther King Sr. and Alberta Williams King for making our way possible. I am also grateful for the ongoing support of my dear sisters-in-law, Coretta Scott King and Naomi Barbour King. They stood by my brothers in the struggle for freedom, raised their children single-handedly, and remain steadfast and true. Finally, I thank those who posed as models for the illustrations: my granddaughter, Farris Christine Watkins, my great nephews, Uriah and Gabriel Ellis; and Ebenezer Baptist Church members, Jethro and Auretha English, Dr. Dolores Robinson, Rev. James Victor, Brenda Davenport, Carl Terry, and Gwendolyn Bunn. I am also appreciative of the creative genius exhibited by the illustrator Chris Soentpiet in visually capturing memorable experiences with my brother Martin. Finally, I wish to thank my editor, Kevin Lewis, for his guidance and helpful suggestions in the preparation of this book.

The publisher thanks Bettman/Corbis for the following photographic references: Profile of Martin Luther King at Massachusetts State Legislature, jacket and page 1; March on Washington, pages 4-5 and 33; "I Have A Dream" speech, page 35. Photographs on front flap and page 39 are from Mrs. Farris's personal collection. All photographs used with permission. We are pleased to include the poem "You Can Be Like Martin" © 1968 by Mildred Johnson published by Mildred Johnson Publications. Used with the author's permission.

 SIMON & SCHUSTER BOOKS FOR YOUNG READERS • An imprint of Simon & Schuster Children's Publishing Division • 1230 Avenue of the Americas, New York, New York 10020
Text copyright © 2003 by Christine King Farris • Illustrations copyright © 2003 by Chris Soentpiet • All rights reserved, including the right of reproduction in whole or in part in any form.
SIMON & SCHUSTER BOOKS FOR YOUNG READERS is a trademark of Simon & Schuster. Book design by Greg Stadnyk
The text for this book is set in Ellington. The illustrations are rendered in watercolor. Manufactured in China • 10 9 8 7 6 5 4 3
Library of Congress Cataloging-in-Publication Data
Farris, Christine King. My brother Martin : a sister remembers growing up with the Rev. Dr. Martin Luther King Jr. / by Christine King Farris ; illustrated by Chris Soentpiet.—1st ed.
p. cm. Summary: Looks at the early life of Martin Luther King Jr., as seen through the eyes of his older sister. ISBN 0-689-84387-9
1. King, Martin Luther, Jr., 1929–1968—Childhood and youth—Juvenile literature. 2. King, Martin Luther, Jr., 1929–1968—Family—Juvenile literature. 3. Farris, Christine King—Juvenile literature. 4. King family—Juvenile literature. 5. African Americans—
Georgia—Atlanta—Social conditions—Juvenile literature. 6. Atlanta (Ga.)—Race relations—Juvenile literature. 7. Atlanta (Ga.)—Biography—Juvenile literature. [1. King, Martin Luther, Jr., 1929–1968—Childhood and youth. 2. Farris, Christine King. 3. King
family. 4. African Americans—Biography.] I. Soentpiet, Chris K., ill. II. Title.
E185.97.K5 F37 2002   323'.092—dc21   2001044681